D0765542

Pills for Cats

Finding Happiness Through Modern Pharmacology

by Charles Kreloff and Patty Brown

Drawings by Victoria Roberts

A Roundtable Press Book

Simon & Schuster

New York   London   Toronto   Sydney   Singapore

For Miso, Caesar, Genvieve & Spike
—C.K. & P.B.

For Huguette Martel
—V.R.

SIMON & SCHUSTER
Rockefeller Center, 1230 Avenue of the Americas, New York, NY 10020

SIMON & SCHUSTER and colophon are registered trademarks of
Simon & Schuster, Inc.

For information regarding special discounts for bulk purchases,
please contact Simon & Schuster Special Sales at 1-800-456-6798 or
business@simonandschuster.com

Designed by Charles Kreloff

Manufactured in Mexico

1   3   5   7   9   10   8   6   4   2

Library of Congress Cataloging-in-Publication Data is available

ISBN 0-7432-6117-8

Pills for Cats

Something had to change.

Fish didn't interest me.

Chicken left me bored.

Drinking from the tap
took too much effort.

For all I cared,
string was string.

Was there no end to my ennui?

I tried self-medicating.

Nibbling catnip, wheatgrass,
and the very expensive topiary
in the living room—
none of them improved
my melancholia.

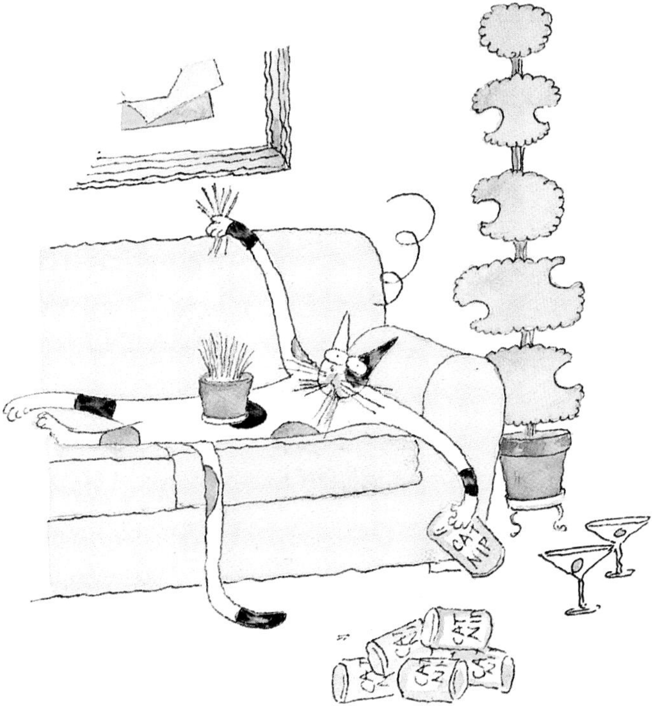
CAT
NIP

Clearly, it was time to seek professional help.

I ended up on the couch.

After a few weeks,
my psychiatrist pulled out
the prescription pad.

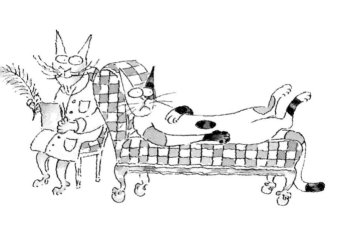

Now I'm a brand-new kitty.

Prozac makes it possible
to float in the pool
like a Portuguese water dog.

One Xanax and
anxious rides to the country
are a thing of the past.

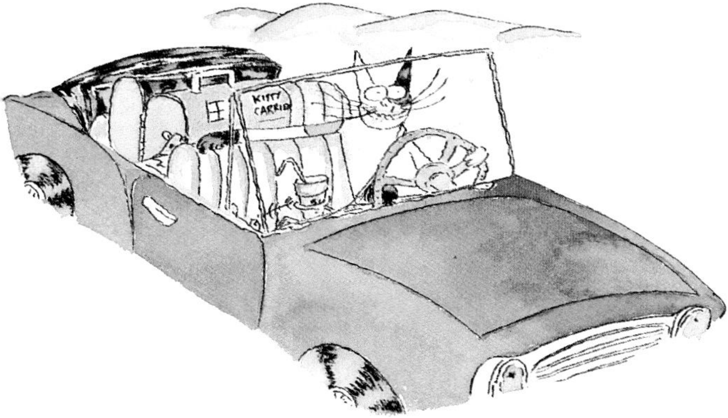
KITTY

On Valium, a visit to the
vet is like a day at the spa.

With Ambien, long flights
are a snooze.

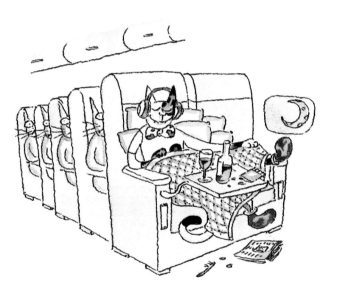

On Klonopin, I could care less about the new kitten.

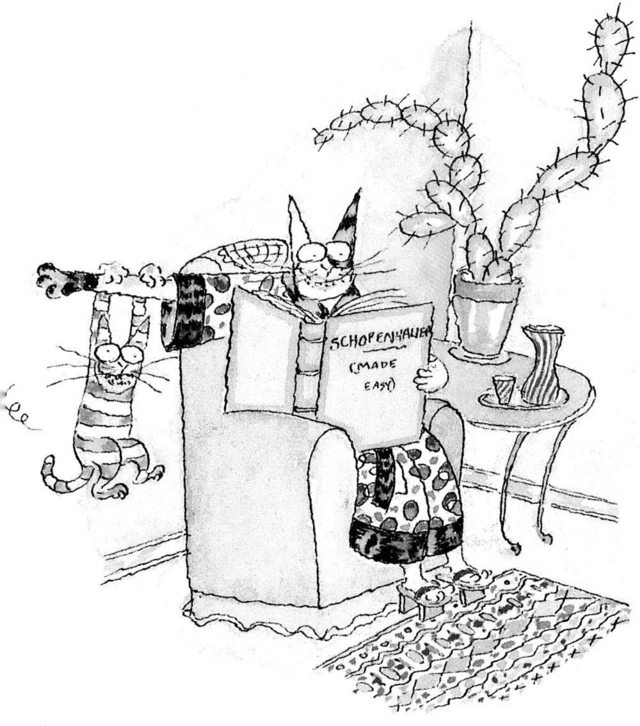
SCHOPENHAUER
(MADE
EASY)

Never a bad first date
with Wellbutrin.

Zoloft calms my
obsessive-compulsive
need to clean.

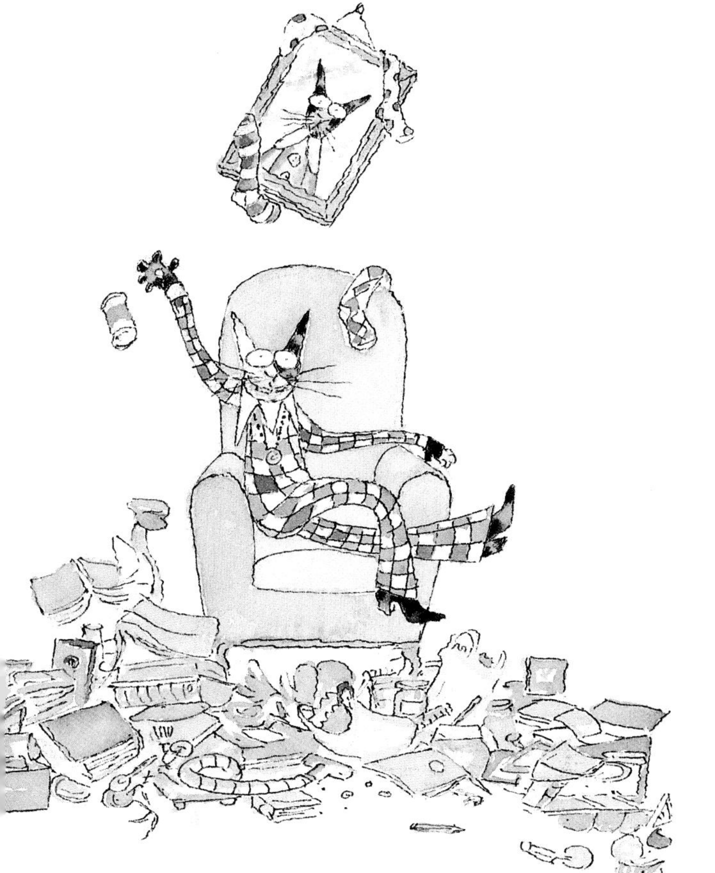

A Viagra or two
comes in handy when
I'm catting around.

What would my family reunion
have been without Paxil?

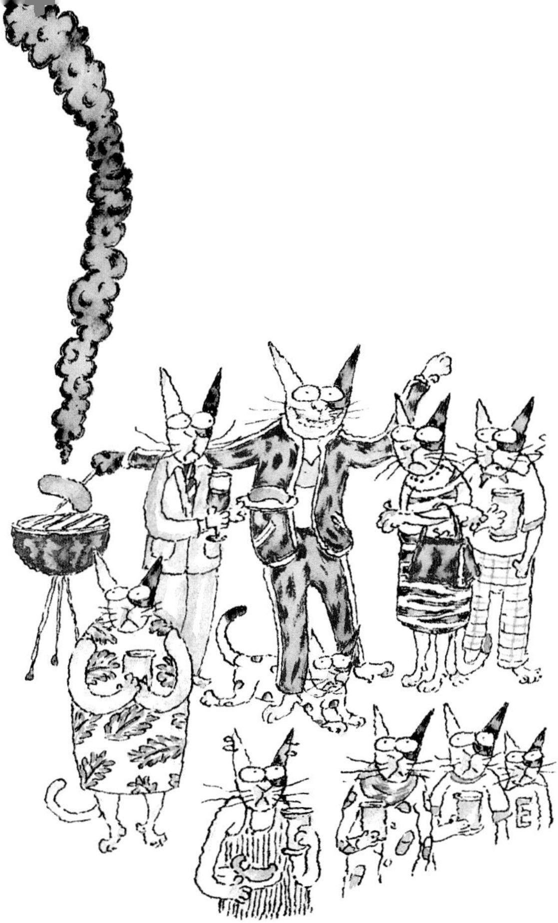
E

With Ritalin, catching anything is a snap.

A bit of Vicodin, and who cares about my bête noire?

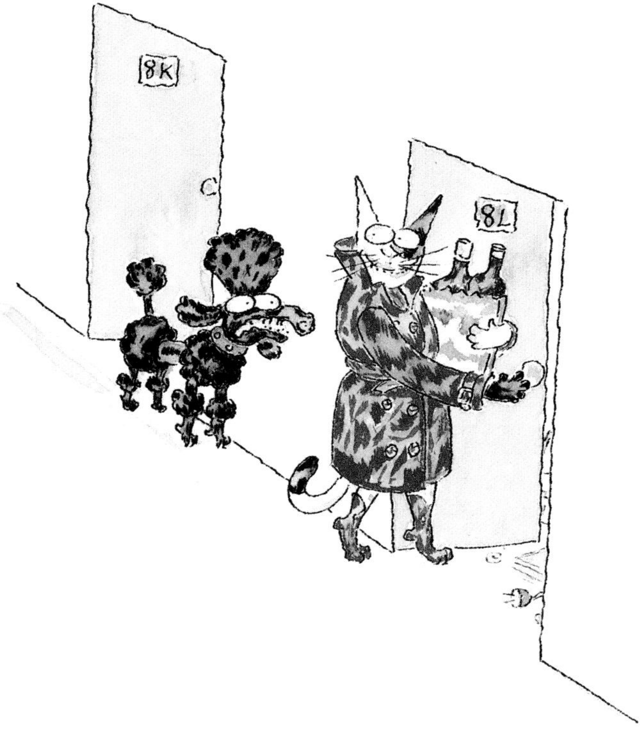
8K
8L

An Ativan relieves my
anal retentiveness.

CAT
TIMES

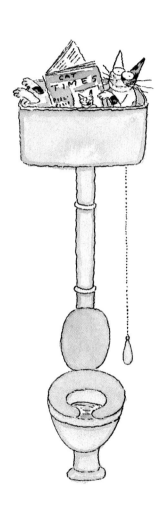

With Elavil, the bon mots aren't the only things flying.

On Percoset there's no shame
when forced to play dress up.

With Adderall, every toy
has its place.

Call me bwana on Celexa.

When in need of a catnap,
one Sonata does the trick.

VALLEY
DOLLS
J. SUSANN

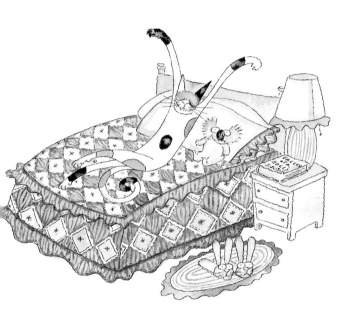

Modern pharmacology has given me a new lease on life.

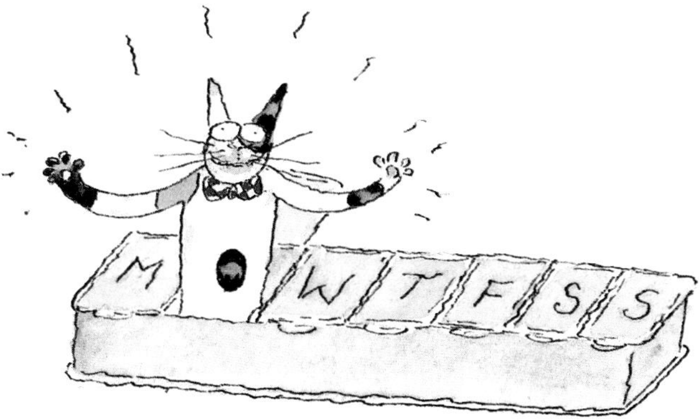
M
W
T
F
S
S

Change is good.